# VOICES of GRIEF

a journey into healing
from the loss of
a loved one

Margaret Dooley Nitka

WovenWord Press

Voices of Grief:
a journey into healing from the loss of a loved one

isbn: 0-9658137-7-0
WovenWord Press
811 Mapleton Avenue
Boulder, Colorado
80304

Copyright
All rights reserved
Book design copyright 1999 Vicki McVey
Cover design copyright 1999 Traci Schalow

# *Acknowledgments*

My mother's life and death were the catalyst for this book. Her legacy has been to call me to look for the greater truth, the deeper meaning. She understood that we stand together as a community and she called us to love and support one another through the pain of her death.

As I have journied on, my own experience of community has been to lean on the incredible strength of family, friends, and fellow pilgrims every step of the way. They have shared their own voices of grief and supplied many insights that I have been blessed to share. I hope that this community understanding of life and death is helpful.

The voices heard within these pages come from those who worship with me, live with me, share their daily lives, births, deaths, triumphs, and failures with me. Their thoughts, words, ideas, and stories have resonated in my life, live in my heart, and grace these pages. Their deep compassion is a mainstay of my idea of our loving Lord. I am deeply grateful for their companionship on the journey.

I offer a very special acknowledgment to the memory of P. Bret Parvin for his beautiful illustrations which I have used as background art for the section pages. Bret listened to my idea for this journal so many years ago, and created these illustrations as his contribution to my work. He has since died, but his interpretations of the symbols of resurrection and life—his butterflies, stars, moon, and dove—will be a living testament to his beautiful spirit.

# *Introduction*

Dear Reader,

This book is about the journey we must take when someone close to us dies. We have never felt so alone, but there is One who is there with each of us when our path through life's journey takes us into the dark country of grief. I found as I faced the long illness and eventual death of my own mother that God was tenderly present all along the way. I came to recognize his presence in the sweet touch of a friend; the sound of a song we had sung together; the sight of morning sunlight glinting on the ocean's waves; the smell of a certain perfume; the taste of a hot dog lunch shared at noon on the boardwalk on a summer's day. I realized that God comforted me using familiar touchstones of my life. In quiet moments he would touch my spirit with a deep peace. He led me gently to know that my mother was safe with him, that she truly lived and dwelt in love with him as she had been born to do.

As I turned to scripture, especially the Psalms, for its comfort and strong poetic images of God's strength and faithfulness, the idea for this bereavement journal came to me. I would choose a passage from the Bible and write it out so I could focus on it through the day. As I went about my daily routines, my experience began to resonate through those holy words. My reflections gave me an overwhelming sense of the presence and comfort of God caring for all of my needs. I began to understand that the coincidence of a friend's presence exactly when I was in need or a rainbow spread across the sky were not random occurrences but the loving acts of a personal God. As I grieved the loss of my mother, I felt his voice grow in my heart and heard words of comfort in my mind that became God's voice of comfort in this journal.

I do not pretend to know how God speaks in another individual's heart, but I know that each one of us holds a unique insight into the profound mystery of God's love for us. This is my insight. It is still a painful task for me to reread and relive my journey of grief through the pages of this journal. God's tenderness and the assurance of his physical, as well as spiritual, presence and comfort were truly there for me. In much the same way as our tender, loving God grieved with me I know he grieves with you.

Before you begin your journey, you may find it helpful to become acquainted with this journal by reading through the entire book. See what lies ahead. There is introductory material, the journal itself, and a section devoted to honoring your loved one and yourself. Choose a starting point that is right for you. Each page is a dialogue of voices: the voice of God speaking through the Scriptures; the voice of the one who mourns; the answering voice of God as he might be heard in the silence of the bereaved person's heart; and the blank space where you may add your own voice.

Many people may find it difficult to respond to this blank space on the page. We may want to do the work which will help us understand ourselves better, but we do not know how. We are not sure we want to put our innermost thoughts on paper at all. Please keep in mind that this journal is yours and yours alone. It need never be shared unless you so choose. Your response at first may even be completely interior. You may want to simply read and meditate on the entries. At your own pace and in your own time, you may then go back and interact on paper. The following suggestions might help you get started on your own journey into healing.

*Time of Day*

It will probably help you to use this book or any other bereavement aids faithfully if you put them into your schedule at a time that makes sense for you. You will want to have privacy and peace. When do you already have some quiet time in your day? Do you work regularly at a desk each day? Is there a time of day or night that is particularly difficult for you that this journal time may help relieve?

*Give Your Entry a Context*

Noting the date will help you to chart your journey when you look back later at your entries. It might also be good for you to jot down anything else of importance to you, for instance: the place, your pet curled up at your feet, the music you are listening to, the thunderstorm outside your window. Any of these facts will help you remember the moment and relate to your feelings at a later date.

*Pen/Pencil/Crayon*

Choose your favorite writing implement and keep it near your journal. Some like the easy flow of ink on paper; others prefer the soft quality of a pencil and the fact that it is not permanent. You may even want to color the illustration that appears with each entry. Let your choice of color tell you about your emotional state. Remember that there is a sense of satisfaction to getting your thoughts and feelings down on paper. Your words may often surprise you. You may set down a fully formed response, write just one word, or draw a picture. The important thing is to be there and be ready for your response.

*Collage*

This is a method of building a picture by cutting and pasting bits of pictures, designs, words, and illustrations from the sympathy cards you may have received, until the collage expresses an idea or feeling. If you don't want to draw or write, try searching for materials that express your emotions and paste them to your journal page. You may choose to layer many objects or place a single item on the page.

*Photographs*

You may want to keep a box of photos nearby which you can look through often and use on your journey. Perhaps, a photo mounted on a page will express your feelings as no words can.

*Notes and Letters*

Don't hesitate to address your loved one in the style of a note or letter. This may be the device you need to free your heart and hand. The practice of communicating in this way may be very helpful in understanding what you are facing as you go on alone.

I ask God's blessing on all who take this journey and I ask you who are bereaved to fall into his arms and trust him to hold you secure.

In his peace and love,
Margaret Dooley Nitka

# Setting Out

*And bowing his head, he handed over his spirit*
John 19:30

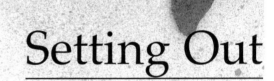

*Voices of Grief*

*May the* LORD *keep watch between you and me when we are out of each other's sight.*
Genesis 31:49

❖ Oh, God, I cry out to you. Where is he? Where has he gone?

❖ *Dear One, I hold him close to my heart. He is in my arms resting for awhile. Give him over to my safekeeping. Together he and I will watch over you.*

*Setting Out*

*There is an appointed time for everything . . .
A time to be born, and a time to die;
a time to plant, and a time to uproot the plant . . .
A time to weep, and a time to laugh;
a time to mourn, and a time to dance.*
    Ecclesiastes 3:1-2, 4

❖ I am like the gnarled trunk of the sycamore outside my winter window. Its stark silhouette is a wound on the snowy landscape. I, too, stand hard and stiff in the harsh winds of mourning. And cold. I am so cold. . . .

❖ *Dear One, the sycamore you gaze at is alive and well in the winter blasts. Its life is drawn down deep inside as it waits to be called forth. My love will continue to flow in your veins and sustain you until you are ready to take up your life and live again.*

*Voices of Grief*

*Can a mother forget her infant,*
*be without tenderness for the child of her womb?*
*Even should she forget, I will never forget.*
Isaiah 49:15

❖ Who holds my little girl as only a mother can?
My arms ache for her small, sweet body.

❖ *My Child, I love her as only a mother can, for it is*
*I who first gave her spirit life. She rests in my strong*
*right arm; with my other arm I reach out for you. She*
*is truly safe here with me and you will come to know*
*that you are safe with me, too.*

4

*The joy of our hearts has ceased,
our dance has turned into mourning.*
Lamentations 5:15

❖ I sway to and fro in a heavy-footed, heavy-hearted mourning dance. My head is down. My arms hang at my sides.

❖ *Dear One, let me be your partner. Let my footsteps go forward for both of us. Lean into my arms. Don't bother to think of the dance. Just let me lead you.*

*Voices of Grief*

*Then he had a dream: a stairway rested on the ground with its top reaching to the heavens; and God's messengers were going up and down on it.*
Genesis 28:12

❖ My dreams are troubled. At night when I close my eyes, I am relieved to let sleep take over my weary brain. But when I wake, the agony of loss I suffer eludes me. Then I remember and I am devastated anew.

❖ *Dear Friend, let my angels renew your strength as you sleep so that your dream time becomes a renewal. I have set my angels to watch over you and to help you bear this burden. Have faith. Take heart from the stairway, the angels and healing dreams.*

*Setting Out*

> *Whatever you ask for in prayer with faith, you will receive.*
> Matthew 21:22

❖ I can't pray. I can't concentrate. But I need desperately to pray. Where are you, God? I need to feel you are here with me in this dark place I have entered.

❖ *Dear One, I am here with you. Do not be troubled about my presence. There are so many ways of reaching me, of praying. Your very thoughts fly directly to my heart. You live in me as you suffer this loss. I know you can't feel my presence now, but when you notice the beauty of a rose or the flash of sunlight on water, I am there. When you feel the gentle touch of a friend, I am there. I am praying with you in these moments..*

*Remove the sandals from your feet, for the place where you stand is holy ground.*
Exodus 3:5

❖ I won't let my feet feel the earth, the very earth where my loved one is buried. They are shod against the hard ground, protected from the chill that rises up, freezes my heart and makes my body tremble.

❖ *Beloved, I invite you to experience my presence in this place. I am here. Take off your shoes and be still. Lift up your head and gaze into my eyes. Feel my power to heal you. Feel the warmth of my love rising up through your body from the very soles of your feet. You are mine and I am yours.*

*Setting Out*

> *All you who are thirsty,*
> *come to the water!*
> Isaiah 55:1

❖ Oh, God, my very spirit is parched. It takes all my strength just to cry out to you.

❖ *Dear Friend, your terrible thirst shall not overcome you. Turn your face up to me. Open your eyes to me. I will rain down healing waters upon you. Let your spirit drink freely of my gifts.*

*Voices of Grief*

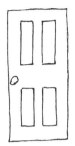
*Ask and it will be given to you; seek and you will find; knock and the door will be opened to you. For everyone who asks, receives; and the one who seeks, finds; and to the one who knocks, the door will be opened.*
Matthew 7:7-9

❖ What is happening to me? I don't have the strength of a child. I need to reach out, to seek others. I need to open the door of my own tomb and step outside to daylight. But I can't. I am so tired, confused. I want only to hide and sleep and not care.

❖ *Rest awhile in me, Dear Friend. It is enough that you recognize the need to open the door. In your own time, when you are ready, you will go forth to continue life's journey. I will be there to help you roll the stone from the entrance to your tomb and walk by your side as you venture forth.*

*Setting Out*

*Are not two sparrows sold for a small coin? Yet not one of them falls to the ground without your Father's knowledge. Even all the hairs of your head are counted. So do not be afraid.*
Matthew 10:29-31

❖ It is summer outside my window. Since his death I have neglected the garden I carefully planted in the spring. It is overgrown now in the heat of July and no longer seems to be mine. Oh, God, this display, this chaos of color and sound which disturbs me so, is your work. These are your flowers, weeds, crickets, grasshoppers, and your sparrows.

❖ *Beloved, I know this garden is an affront to you in your deep sorrow. Let it remind you that you are the most precious of my creatures. I have listened to your hopes and dreams. I know your heart and you are mine.*

*Voices of Grief*

> *You shall not fear the terror of the night*
> *nor the arrow that flies by day.*
> Psalm 91:5

❖ I am so frightened of this unknown. It seems that all I can think of, all I dream about, is death. I fear the shadows in the hall at night. I fear the deafening ticking of the clock by day. I wake from fitful sleep with my heart pounding in my chest.

❖ *Quiet, quiet, Beloved. Allow me to surround you with my gentle love. Do not let the shadows engulf you. It doesn't seem possible to you now, but all will be well again one day. I have drawn both of you close. She is with me and prays as constantly for you as you do for her. Be still now and rest in this knowledge. I am with you, holding you, always.*

*Deep waters cannot quench love,
nor floods sweep it away.*
Song of Songs 8:7

❖ I long to see the one I have lost. Why do I live while he is gone from this earth? My body drives me forward seeking nourishment, water, sleep. But my heart wails for yesterday, for the days when we laughed and sang in the sun.

❖ *Dear One, stand before me and receive my blessing. Just for today, let my love flow into your heart and fill you with my peace. Let tomorrow take care of itself. You are precious to me. Refresh yourself in me and you will begin to heal your suffering spirit. Remember, my love for you will never die.*

*Voices of Grief*

*At the sight of the crowds, his heart was moved with pity for them because they were troubled and abandoned, like sheep without a shepherd.*
Matthew 9:36

❖ Mary's funeral was today. We had coffee at her house on Tuesday. Thursday she had her hair appointment. On Friday, Mary was in an automobile accident. By Saturday, she was gone. My calendar book for tomorrow says, "Mary. Lunch. 12:30" Oh, God, my best friend is gone. How can this be? We did everything together.

❖ *Dear Friend, we are truly united as we mourn Mary's death. I watched over you as you joined with that sad circle of friends and family. I watch over you as you sit here alone and remember her. Please go on being my hands and heart as you were so many times with Mary. Have lunch tomorrow in her honor. Gather your friends together and I will be there with Mary in your midst, encouraging you all to go on.*

*Setting Out*

*The* LORD*, your God, has directed all your journeying in the desert.*
Deuteronomy 8:2

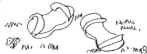

❖ I wander aimlessly. I pray and I hear no answering voice, only the sound of my own. I lift my eyes and see no one standing near. My heart is barren and dry as the desert.

❖ *Dear One, even in the desert there is the oasis of my love. You are moving toward my refreshing shade and cool, sweet water. Do not give up. As you walk on, you will find rest in my arms.*

*Voices of Grief*

*My soul is sorrowful even to death. Remain here and keep watch with me.*
Matthew 26:38

❖ My family is smothering me with their approach to her death. They expect everyone to keep up a united front of self control. They've banished her as a person because remembering and facing her death is too painful. I know I can't go on like this.

❖ *Beloved, yield to your grief. Let your tears flow. Tell the stories of her life. Draw your strength from her. Gently tell them she lives forever and that she is still with them, but in a new and more powerful way. I will remain with you and keep watch. You shall not bear your sorrow alone.*

*Setting Out*

*He took away our infirmities
and bore our diseases.*
Matthew 8:17

❖ Oh, God, we begged for healing yet she suffered and died. Her disease seemed to bind us together in horror. It was a hell on earth. Those days of suffering gripped my heart and still hold it in an icy grasp.

❖ *Dear Friend, my healing came in those who touched you during her illness. They brought dinner, prayed, told stories, sent cards, and quietly formed a circle of love around you. Yes, I heard your prayer and was present among you. I held each of you in my arms as I held her. When you embrace each other now, I am there. Let her dying time be a pathway to the heaven where she abides with me.*

*Voices of Grief*

> *He said to them, "It is I. Do not be afraid."*
> John 6:20

❖ I raised him alone. There was nothing I wouldn't do for him; now there is nothing I can do for him. I have given him up to an unknown world. Who there will know and love him as I did?

❖ *My Child, you have not yet realized how deeply I inhabit your life. I am everywhere you are. It is I who love you beyond human comprehension. It is I who seek you. He rests here with me and has no fear. Let the love you have known in your earthly life together continue to lead you to me.*

*Setting Out*

*The L<small>ORD</small> bless you and keep you!*
*The L<small>ORD</small> let his face shine upon you, and be gracious to you!*
*The L<small>ORD</small> look upon you kindly and give you peace.*
Numbers 6:24-26

❖ We both loved the close, peaceful moments when he would climb into my lap and ask me to read a story. Oh my God, I will never read to him again. . . .

❖ *Dearest, I gather your anguished being, body and soul, up in my arms. I weep with you over this separation. I long to find ways to comfort you and give you my peace. Please take this time of pain and turn toward me. I will hold you both close and shower you with my grace.*

*Voices of Grief*

*After I have been raised up, I shall go before you to Galilee.*
Matthew 26:32

❖ I believe she'll be happy with you forever, my God. But I look at her things and can't control my tears. My faith seems useless today. Have I lost this, too?

❖ *Dear Heart, these tears are for you. You have lost the intimacy of your daily human relationship. Your heart must express such a deep loss and wash its bitterness from your spirit. I have experienced everything you are suffering. Know that I set out on the same journey when I walked the earth. I feel your pain and I will not leave you alone. I live and she lives with me.*

*I will raise him on the last day.*
John 6:44

❖ It's out of my hands. The prescription bottles, never to be finished, sit on the bedside table. I woke every two hours tonight as usual, Lord, to see that he was comfortable, to give him a sip of water. I am torturing myself with the very routine that comforted him. In a strange way, though, I feel that I am still keeping watch over him. In the lonely night I am remembering his name.

❖ *My Child, I hear your voice crying out in the silence of the night. His name is written in the book of life. Commend him to my care. He lives in joy and no longer suffers. I hold you close, too, so you can feel the loving beat of my heart.*

*Voices of Grief*

> *For see, the winter is past,*
> *the rains are over and gone.*
> *The flowers appear on the earth.*
> Song of Songs 2:11-12

❖ Flowers are out of place in my gray landscape. They speak of funerals to me. Instead of life and love, roses now say death and loss to me.

❖ *Dear Friend, draw hope from the flowers that your heart will bloom again in its own time. Abide with me while we wait for this miracle. I will watch with you for your springtime.*

*Setting Out*

*I see people looking like trees and walking.*
Mark 8:24

❖ I sit here in the front pew, God. I'm surrounded by people I love . . . aunts, uncles, cousins, friends. Everyone is here but one special person. He lies in a draped coffin next to us in the center aisle. I am not even sure how I got here. Who chose my clothing? Who clasped the pearls he gave me around my neck?

❖ *Beloved, I see your confusion and pain. Your life is suddenly changed and you hardly know which way to turn in your agony. Turn to me. I will heal your blindness. You will know that I am next to you in the front row and you will see clearly with the perfect vision of your Father, God.*

*Voices of Grief*

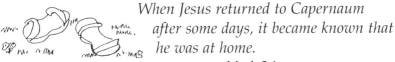

> When Jesus returned to Capernaum after some days, it became known that he was at home.
> Mark 2:1

❖ There in hard, cold type was his obituary notice. There were the precious letters of his name with the facts of his life. Is that what it comes down to, Lord? I would have mentioned his compassion, his commitment to family and friends, his untiring service to all, his gentle sense of humor, his kindness and patience. He made a home, a welcome, a dwelling place for all in his heart.

❖ *My Child, your dear one is at home resting with me. The facts of his life are simple . . . he loved and was loved in return. His spirit now lives in the source of all compassion, commitment, service, humor, kindness, and patience. His love reaches out to you and bids you follow him home.*

*Setting Out*

*Jesus said, "Someone has touched me; for I know that power has gone out from me."*
Luke 8:46

❖ Oh God, I hope they don't stop touching us. I am writing thank you notes for all the sympathy and love showered on us since she died. The words I use are so ordinary. They are incapable of expressing the depth of my gratitude. I need the doorbell to chime, the phone to ring, a note to arrive, a covered dish to be left on our front door step. Our family has never been in such desperate need. We can't seem to go on by ourselves.

❖ *Dear One, so many are praying for you. They pray with their hearts and their hands. In their touch is my power to heal. It surrounds, uplifts, and protects you in your time of need.*

*Voices of Grief*

*If a house is divided against itself, that house will not be able to stand.*
Mark 3:25

❖ Everyone had a different approach to his life-threatening illness . . . travel to a world famous hospital, diet and nutrition, alternative medicine. He wanted only peace and the comfort of home, family, and friends. Finally, he gathered us together and quietly asked for our blessing and support to continue his battle in his own way. He died soon after, amid peace and prayer. Thank you, God, that he was able to bring us back together. At least we still have each other.

❖ *Precious Friend, you gave him the freedom and strength to let go of his earthly life. He knew that he needed all of your joined hands to help him come home to me. He in turn gave you back the strength of one another to cope with his death.*

*Father, if you are willing, take this cup away from me; still, not my will but yours be done.*
Luke 22:42

❖ The wind howls in a wicked winter storm tonight. Its blasts pierce my body and my heart. How have I come even this far, Lord? Will you walk with me and guard me against this wind?

❖ *Dear One, with me beside you, you are much stronger than you know. You have the strength of the God of all creation to draw upon. Together we shall stand up to the cold winds of your grief.*

*Voices of Grief*

> *Today you will be with me in Paradise.*
> Luke 23:43

❖ Promises. Everyone is telling me they will be in touch; that I must call them any time. It is quiet now. I am all alone and I don't know how to reach out. I am totally alone.

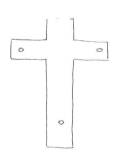

❖ *I have entered your life in a new way now, My Friend. I have made promises to you that you can trust in. Remember, I am as close as your next breath. I will live with you through many people. I will walk through your door, sit at your table. And whenever you need me, day or night, I will hear you. Fear not, I will never leave you alone.*

*Jesus wept.*
John 11:35

❖ When I think of God at all, I think of an all powerful, majestic king, an eternal being shrouded in mystery. But now I know he is also the God who wept. He lost his friend just as I lost my friend.

❖ *Oh, yes, Dear One, I understand how it is to turn and look for someone who is no longer there. Remember that I raised my friend, Lazarus, from the dead and I shall do the same for all of my friends.*

*Voices of Grief*

> *Naked, I came forth from my mother's womb,*
> *and naked shall I go back again!*
> *The LORD gave and the LORD has taken away;*
> *blessed be the name of the LORD.*
> Job 1:21

❖ She was the mother of one, grandmother of eight, great grandmother of ten. She was blind and deaf and could be reached only by stroking the silky skin of her arm or cheek. Sometimes she responded peacefully, but at other times she became agitated and lashed out. God, it is so painful to remember her this way.

> ❖ *Beloved, remember her as I see her. Her blue eyes twinkled and her hands could never do enough for you. She loved to sit with you over a cup of tea and delighted in holding her great grandchildren in her arms. Remember her for her life giving. Remember her for her love.*

# Along the Way

*The sun will be darkened,
and the moon will not give its light.*
Mark: 13:24

*Voices of Grief*

*I set my bow in the clouds to serve as a sign of the covenant between me and the earth.*
Genesis 9:13

❖ Dear God, you know me. I find reassurance in the simple things of life . . . a birthday card, a phone call, a coffee break shared with a friend. Please send me a sign of your love to ease the steps of my journey today.

❖ *Child, sometimes my embrace gets lost in the rush of the day. Just today I gave you a sudden feeling of well-being, of warmth deep inside you as you watched the wild geese fly overhead. Remember? You noticed the good feeling, but didn't realize I was the one who held you close. Just be still and listen for my presence as you walk through your day. I am there with you. I made a covenant with you when I died for you on the cross. I know you and I love you.*

*Along the Way*

> *Unless a grain of wheat falls to the ground and dies, it remains just a grain of wheat; but if it dies, it produces much fruit.*
> John 12:24

❖ Lord, I was forced to let go. My life is empty now, but my heart feels too full of emotion. I begin to cry at the slightest thing . . . the sight of someone who seems painfully familiar, the sound of a voice that I thought for a moment was hers. I know she would want me to understand my feelings and reach out to others. Please help me to do this.

❖ *If you do, Dear One, you will notice the tender shoot that life yearns to send forth. Till the soil. Water the earth with your tears. Pour your feelings upon the little plot I have given you to tend in this life, and one day you will notice the tiny green plant. It is life itself bursting forth from the dark earth. Your loved one is living on in you and me.*

*Voices of Grief*

*Come to me, all you who labor and are burdened, and I will give you rest. Take my yoke upon you and learn from me, for I am meek and humble of heart; and you will find rest for yourselves. For my yoke is easy, and my burden light.*
Matthew 11:28-30

❖ Tomorrow is our wedding anniversary, but she is gone. Her chair is empty. I eat alone. Her knitting lies untouched. There is no one beside me when I turn my head to receive her reassurance, her smile, her look of deep love. Please grant me the grace of remembering the joy of her loving presence especially at this time of my loneliness.

❖ *Precious Friend, I share your burden. I place the yoke of your pain about my neck and shoulders and lift you up. Know that in my strength you will find rest and the courage to go on. Now, breathe deeply, slowly. Recognize my strong presence as you feel the life-giving, soothing flow of my breath enter your innermost being.*

*The people who sit in darkness
have seen a great light,
on those dwelling in a land overshadowed by death
light has arisen.*
Matthew 4:16

❖ Today I met another person who is suffering as I am. She let me say his name. She didn't tell me I *should* feel better or I *would* feel better or it was time to move on with life. She just listened. I cried with her and felt the crushing load of grief lighten.

❖ *Dear Heart, I will send many people to help you through the night of your grief. Trust in me. It was my love that held you both today. In her hand you touched mine; in her spirit you knew me; in her strength you found my strength to help you bear your sorrow.*

*Voices of Grief*

> *Jesus turned around and saw her, and said, "Courage, daughter! Your faith has saved you."*
> Matthew 9:22

❖ Oh, God, I relied on him so. He was strong and sure in his decisions, his leadership of our family. I want to call upon the example of his strength so I can be truly supportive the way he was. I want to rely on you, heavenly father, so they can begin to rely on me.

❖ *My Child, he drew his strength from me. Now it is your turn. Place your fearful heart in my hands. Courage, daughter, I am here to help you. I stand next to you, behind you, over you, beneath your feet. I am with you in every way. Have no fear. Accept my gift of strength and faith.*

*Jesus looked at them and said, "For human beings this is impossible, but for God all things are possible."*
Matthew 19:26

❖ I spend my time hammering, sanding, and sawing. The only way I seem to silence the voice of grief inside my head is to keep my hands busy. I want to come to the place where my heart is in my work again, too, and that will take time. At least my pounding and rasping results in building something new. I must hang on and continue with my life.

❖ *For me all things are possible, Dear One. Be quiet for a moment and listen for my voice. You can do anything with me. You are passing through the fear, the numbness, the bitterness, the shocking pain of death. But I will lead you through it into life. Hammering and pounding are ways to release your fear and anger and, eventually, let them go. I will be with you through it all.*

*Voices of Grief*

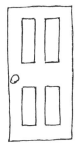

> *May you be blessed in your coming in,*
> *and blessed in your going out!*
> Deuteronomy 28:6

❖ Inside my house, all is in order. I'm torn between the refuge that is my house and the need to get into the outside world where I feel so vulnerable to the sights, sounds, and smells of the neighborhood we shared. Sometimes I hungrily tread the paths of memory; sometimes I push away the images of the times we shared. I'm so afraid I'll forget and in the forgetting, he will truly be lost from me.

❖ *Beloved, no one I have called into life will ever be forgotten. He lives on with me for all eternity. His dwelling place is one of light and peace. Keep your precious memories of him alive. But draw true comfort from the knowledge that I hold him close and protect him from all harm. In time, you will know peace again. I hold you, too, in my sheltering love. I will bless your every breath and effort to open the door to your life.*

*I will rescue you by my outstretched arm.*
Exodus 6:6

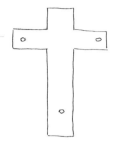

❖ I am crying again. There is no one here with me to comfort me. No strong arms will encircle me to quiet my tears. My friends say I need to accept their loving concern for me. I need to let go and allow them to comfort me. I want to tell them that with their help I will be all right.

❖ *Precious Friend, I know your pain and I am aware of your grief. We are united in the deepest of mysteries . . . life, death, and the love that binds us closely together through it all. Remember that I stretched out my arms for you once on the cross and I will not forsake you now. Let your friends embrace you and we will go on together.*

*Voices of Grief*

> *Know that I am with you; I will protect you wherever you go, and bring you back to this land.*
> Genesis 28:15

❖ I want to pack my bag and run away. But where would I go? Everyone close to me, even my youngest sister, is gone. We lived together for so many years that we relied on each other completely. I thought I couldn't go on but when I got out of bed this morning, I suddenly remembered the cheerful smile she started each day with and I realized she's still with me. As I put my slippers on, I knew I could put one foot in front of the other today.

❖ *Dear One, you are not alone. We all walk with you, protecting you and preparing you for your own entry into my promised land. There is still much for you to do for yourself and for others on your journey. Go to those around you and let them love you for me. In time, you will be able to reach out to the ones whose feet falter from loneliness and your own burden will be lightened.*

*Along the Way*

*But whence can wisdom be obtained,
and where is the place of understanding.*
Job 28:12

❖ I read about a bereavement ministry today. Could there be a place for me in this group? I don't know if a support group is right for me, but it would be a place to tell my story, to say his name, to just talk about his death. It would be a place for me to go.

❖ *My Dear Child, even I had the support of a group when I walked our beloved earth. My close friends listened to me and I listened to them. We talked about our hopes and dreams. We talked about life and death. Our Father God was present there among us. He will be with you, too, as you try to discover meaning in this time of your life.*

*He reached out from on high and grasped me;
he drew me out of deep waters.*
2 Samuel 22:17

❖ Hands reached out to me today. Bob shook my hand this morning at Mass; Tom gave me a pat on the back. Elaine held my hand as she told me that her granddaughter, Emma, had taken her first step. Then little Emma herself reached her arms out to me and climbed right up into my lap. She hugged me and seemed to know I needed her love.

❖ *Beloved Friend, I sent all of those friends to reach out to you today. I know it's hard for you to let people into your quiet world. Did you notice their smiles as you responded to each warm affirmation? You are important to these people in your life. Be warmed by their hands. Be comforted by the wonder of my eternal love offered by even the smallest of hands.*

*Along the Way*

*When the Lord saw her, he was moved with pity
for her and said to her, "Do not weep."*
Luke 7:13

❖ Will my tears ever dry up? Where do they come from in such an unending river? I only know I need them now for, somehow, I am calmer after they storm through my body. I never thought I would thank you, God, for this gift of tears.

❖ *Dear Heart, tears are your oldest emotional language. I gave them to you when you were a newborn baby. You had tears before you had any other means of communication. Tears were your way of expressing your deepest needs, of calling for comfort and love. Let someone hold you and dry your tears. I will be there with you.*

*Voices of Grief*

*Have you seen him whom my heart loves?*
Song of Songs 3:3

❖ Hurrying home from work today, I thought I saw him walking up ahead of me on the sidewalk. The surging crowd of pedestrians parted for a moment and he seemed to be there. I saw that familiar stride and set of the shoulders and I raised my hand and started to call his name. Oh, God, my heart rose so high and fell so low all in that instant. Please take care of him for me.

❖ *My Child, love knows no boundaries. You two were united on earth and so you are united in me. He still walks up ahead of you, preparing a place for you in the kingdom.*

*Along the Way*

*Martha, Martha, you are anxious and worried
about many things.*
Luke 10:41

❖ God, I devoted all my energy to running the household. So often when I might have been praying, listening, loving him, I was consumed with daily details: dinner, laundry, homework, car pools. Now I understand that behind all the details there is your quiet presence in my life. In those moments I believe you are giving me the gift of your peace.

❖ *Beloved Friend, don't look at the past and live in the things you'd like to change. I know the care you lavished on your family and all who came to you. I know the love you gave was unselfish. Now the days stretch out before you. Turn to me and focus your attention. I am knocking; please open the door of your heart to me.*

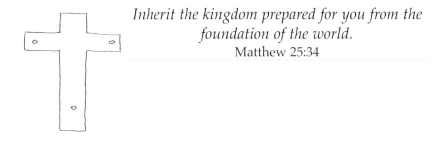

*Inherit the kingdom prepared for you from the foundation of the world.*
Matthew 25:34

❖ My husband was truly faith-filled. On a Sunday morning he would happily anticipate attending Mass, followed by Sunday breakfast and the newspapers. I went to Mass with him every Sunday, but I didn't have the same gift of faith he had. How ironic that I now kneel here alone and feel my faith begin to grow. I hope that he will find me here and whisper a word of encouragement the way he always did. The shaft of sunlight that used to fall on his shoulder and touch his hair with light fell on me today. I cried when I felt its warmth.

❖ *Dear Heart, Sunday after Sunday you seek him here. What great faith you have that he lives! The sunlight that bathed you this morning was his gift to you. My gift to you is eternal life in a place of never-ending light and love.*

*Along the Way*

*Do not weep any longer, for she is not dead, but sleeping.*
Luke 8:52

❖ My role as father was to be strong . . . breadwinner, protector, disciplinarian. I had no fears, no questions, no doubts. But the only faith I had was in myself. Oh, God, now my heart understands that you are my father and hers, too. Your fatherhood is all-loving, and I know that I can trust in your care for her and for me.

❖ *Dear Friend, when she came to me she brought her love for you with her. Her falling asleep has awakened you. Your daughter lives on in me. Let her presence in your life continue to bless you. Let her help you grow closer to me with each passing day.*

*Voices of Grief*

> *Destroy this temple and in three days I will raise it up.*
> John 2:19

❖ It hurt so much to stand by my friend as he suffered. When I was young I learned that our bodies are temples of the Holy Spirit, and watching my friend I wondered if God could dwell in that ravaged body. Then I saw how much love he gave to all of us at his bedside, and I knew God was dwelling there. Now when I think of my friend, I don't remember his pain; I remember the love that flowed out of him.

❖ *My Child, the beautiful body I created for him in his mother's womb was destroyed. But no disease was able to erase my presence in him. As his body diminished, he invited my love to grow in him until I penetrated every relationship, every aspect of his life. Couldn't you feel his love for you burning in his outstretched hand, his smile of welcome, his pleasure when you read to him? His whole body became fuel for the flame of my peace, love, and joy. Today he shines in glory with me.*

*Along the Way*

> *Master, to whom shall we go? You have the words of eternal life.*
> John 6:68

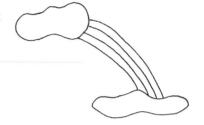

❖ Words, words, words. Reading a mystery, which was my greatest escape before, has turned into a chore. I can't seem to keep the characters straight. I just don't care the way I used to. Maybe now I understand how precious time is and I don't want to waste a moment. Perhaps this is something I'm beginning to learn.

❖ *My Dear Friend, escape to me and cling to my words. They are the simplest and most powerful words you will ever need to hear: I love you; I am here for you; I will never leave you.*

*Voices of Grief*

 *For God so loved the world that he gave his only Son, so that everyone who believes in him might not perish but might have eternal life.*
John 3:16

❖ She was my only daughter, a wonderful young woman and fearless. For one who was so sensitive to injustice and human hurt to die the victim of a crime is an outrage! She dreamed of saving the world. Now I am trying to understand her vision. I find myself being stretched and growing toward the world she wanted to save. In a way, I'm closer to her now than ever.

❖ *Dear Heart, in the quiet of your spirit you will feel her gentle presence. Her unselfish love and care for others was learned in the heart of your family life. She lives now with me and prepares a place for you. Walk each day in the way that you taught her and come at last into my eternal embrace.*

*Jesus stopped and called them and said, "What do you want me to do for you?" They answered him, "Lord, let our eyes be opened."*
Matthew 20:32-33

❖ I want the nightmare to end. I want to do ordinary things like bake him chocolate chip cookies and kiss him good night. I want him alive and breathing and singing and crying and laughing. I want to look into his eyes again. . . . At least now I am able to understand what a gift he was to me and I thank my God for him every day.

❖ *Beloved, if you let me I will open your eyes. I will show you how much I love you. I will give you companions to walk at your side and help you bear the pain. As you journey along, you will see my tender concern for you that is beyond all human understanding. Just keep your eyes and your heart focused on me.*

*Voices of Grief*

*Do not worry about tomorrow; tomorrow will take care of itself.*
Matthew 6:34

❖ I feel that I am living in yesterday and tomorrow. God, you know I always had trouble with living in the moment. And now such silence surrounds me! Please fill my moments with your voice, your presence, and your purpose for my life. Help me to know you are there.

❖ *Reach out, Dear Heart. Listen to my voice in the silence. Each day is a precious new gift. Each moment of today you live and move and have your being in me, your God. When I send someone to you with a smile and a hug, draw strength from those gestures of love. When a soft breeze touches your cheek, take comfort for I have sent it to soothe your spirit. Be gentle with yourself today. You are loved beyond any measure of time or human love.*

*Along the Way*

*While he was at table in his house, many tax collectors and sinners sat with Jesus and his disciples; for there were many who followed him.*
Mark 2:15

❖ Her cheerful, orderly routine of days and nights is over for us now. She is gone. These long months I have been in a trance with my eyes fixed on the beautiful life she created for us. I know now her love was your gift to me. I want to find a way to give something back in her memory.

 ❖ My Dear Child, life is my gift to you. I am the God of your former, peaceful life and I am the God of your present upheaval. I await you among the bereaved and the joyful, the sick and the healthy, the tax collectors, sinners, and disciples. I wait patiently at your side for the day when you will take your place at my table and rejoin the feast of life I have prepared for you.

*Voices of Grief*

*Of its own accord the land yields fruit, first the blade,
then the ear, then the full grain in the ear.*
Mark 4:28

❖ God, I have been noticing lately that the knife-pain of my grief has become a dull ache. Where my heart should calmly beat in my chest, there is only a wounded place of hurt and emptiness. It is a physical sensation, my ever-present companion. But the sharp pain that made me cry out at night is gone and I think you are calling me to make room for something new.

❖ *Dear Friend, it is the way of all creation to heal itself, to grow to wholeness and completion. The seed of life lies within you and will begin to germinate in the dark shelter of your suffering spirit. This ache is a sign of new life, conceived and born in your pain. In this process lies your healing and through it you will become whole again.*

*Along the Way*

*I do believe, help my unbelief!*
Mark 9:24

❖ Another long night of tossing and turning. My hair is knotted on my crumpled pillow. A dream image of a dark house flashes across my mind's eye. Its doors stand open, curtains blow out of the upstairs windows. I want to close the windows and doors and turn on the lights. I want soft light to bathe the walls and floors, like the sun shining on my childhood drawings of our family home.

❖ *Dear One, your faith is calling you home, back to the person you are, deep within your soul. You have struggled long and valiantly and you are ready to sweep the shadows from the rooms of your heart. Each day you come closer to trusting your faith in me and your ability to live in that faith again.*

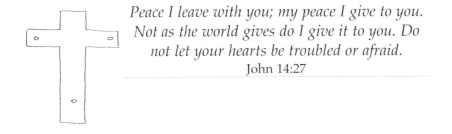

*Peace I leave with you; my peace I give to you. Not as the world gives do I give it to you. Do not let your hearts be troubled or afraid.*
John 14:27

❖ God, I exist in a state of constant inner conflict. Harsh reality has set in. Now I truly know my cold bed will remain cold. I know I will sit alone in church on Sunday. I will pay the bills and make decisions around the house amid storms of anxiety. But I realize now that our son and daughter have been trying to share the burden with me all along. Thank you for them. May I be there for them, too, as I learn to accept their help.

❖ *Dear Friend, in the course of your grieving it is necessary for your anger and fear to surface. Abide in me and this will become a healing time for you. I faced the terror of the cross with the help of my Father. Take my hand and I will guide you through your fear. Rely on me in your prayer to be there with you. Let my peace wash over your spirit and sink into your soul.*

*For behold, the kingdom of God is among you.*
Luke 17:21

❖ I sit at my desk each morning. Turn on my computer. Respond to my email. Go to my meetings. Write my reports. Turn off my light and thank God for the end of another day. Then, I start all over again the next morning. Please, Lord, help me to find the meaning in all this again.

❖ *Dear One, your day is structured by work that seems to have been stripped of all meaning. But as you meet each day's challenges and perform its tasks, you will be surviving and even growing. Remember, your world is my world. I dwell deep within you and within each person you meet. Remain open to me. Allow my work of healing you to go on within your daily routine of work.*

*Voices of Grief*

*"We played the flute for you, but you did not dance.
We sang a dirge, but you did not weep."*
Luke 7:32

❖ What does everyone expect of me? I try so hard not to be too sad around my friends. They tell me, "that's better!" when they see me smile. I'm trying so hard to be alive to their love, to life.

❖ *Dear Child, they care about you so very much. It is human for them to be so fearful of death. They want you to return to life healed of your grief. Lean on them and don't give up. Lean on others, too, who share your experience of grief and understand you need time to return to the dance of life. Remember, I will wait for your dancing; I will hold you in your weeping.*

*I will not leave you orphans; I will come to you.*
John 14:18

❖ God, I am an orphan. I may be a middle-aged woman with grown children of my own, but mother's death made me an orphan. I guess my mother's love was very close to the way you love me. Her love was as unconditional as an earthly love can be; yours is truly unconditional forever. I am beginning to see that she is completely safe and at rest in your arms. Thank you for helping me understand this.

❖ *Dear Child, her love was a mirror of my love. You have my promise that you are not orphans, but my own children. Her love has taught you how to love others.*

*Voices of Grief*

*I am the gate. Whoever enters through me will be saved, and will come in and go out and find pasture.*
John 10:9

❖ My thoughts of a family I encountered while grocery shopping today are so painful to me. Grandmother pushed granddaughter in the shopping cart, while mother selected their favorite cookies. They were laughing and playing together. They reminded me so much of our own happy times not so long ago. I wanted to tell them not to waste a single second.

❖ *Dear One, the intense emotions of your grief cannot separate us. When you are ready, it will be through me that you find your way back to peace. Your grief is as deep as the pain of your loss. That loss will always remain in your heart, but you will be able to let the pain go. Trust that you will continue your own journey toward me and that you will come to understand the loving freedom of my open gate.*

*Along the Way*

*On this mountain he will destroy the veil that veils all people.*
Isaiah 25:7

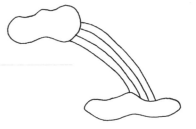

❖ I live in a different land now. I struggle daily through tangled briars, muddy bogs and dark threatening forests. At times the way seems easier, almost level. Then I plunge again into fear and uncertainty. I seem to carry a heavy pack of concerns on my shoulder, but I have come to realize that you are there to share my burden. Now my challenge is to trust that you are there so I can let go of the weight I am trying to carry by myself.

❖ *Beloved, sooner or later everyone crosses the border into this land. The mists of ordinary life with its thousands of minute details swirl about and obscure the landscape. Then one day the air clears and you can finally see that heaven and earth are separated by a mere heartbeat, a single breath. You are so close to the mountaintop, the land of the living. Take my hand and we will continue the journey together.*

# Coming Home

*I am the way and the truth and the life.*
John 14:6

*Our Father in heaven,
hallowed be your name,
your kingdom come,
your will be done,
on earth as in
heaven.*
Matthew 6:9-10

❖ I find myself feeling closer than ever to my father now that he has died. It started soon after his death . . . this feeling of his love surrounding me. As the days and months have passed by, my certainty grows that my dear father lives on with Our Father in heaven.

❖ *Dear Friend, I created him, breathed the breath of life into him, called him by name to live with me through all eternity. Then I gave him to you. The small hands he held were yours; the bicycle he steadied, the swings he pushed, were all for you. His father love came from my heart and continues to flow into yours. You two are one in my love.*

*Voices of Grief*

*I command you: be firm and steadfast! Do not fear nor be dismayed, for the LORD, your God, is with you wherever you go.*
Joshua 1:9

❖ This winter afternoon, I draw the fire of the setting sun deep within my soul. Many evenings have I glanced out my window and gazed with sadness at the daily dying of the light. But today's sunset is a glowing gold witness to God's presence in all creation. It whispered 'peace' to me. Suddenly, I needed to stand in this healing light. I know the sunset reached into my frozen heart and touched off a small spark of hope there.

❖ *Beloved Friend, I am so pleased that you walked out into my gift of evening. Your nightly vigil at the window has not escaped my notice. You have been reaching towards my benediction at day's end, but tonight you embraced the setting sun and allowed the golden rays into your heart. To life!*

*Wherever you die I will die, and there be buried.*
Ruth 1:17

❖ I kneel at her grave and wish I could see her actually rise up in front of me. I know I must be content with the memory of her smile, her walk, the way she inclined her head toward me as she listened. I picture her in her white dress on a summer's day walking on the beach. My heart catches at the loveliness of the memory. I am deeply grateful that such a wonderful person lived and breathed at my side.

❖ *Dear One, I share your peaceful presence . . . the beauty of your memory, the simplicity of a prayer whispered at grave side. You kneel on the sacred ground which marks your beloved's final resting place. The earth is my garden and she blooms among my flowers. My peace be with you.*

*Voices of Grief*

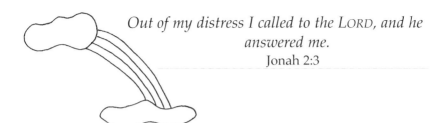

*Out of my distress I called to the* LORD, *and he answered me.*
Jonah 2:3

❖ There was a horrible rain squall today. As I drove through the storm, I felt an overwhelming sadness and cried out to God, "Help me! Are you really there? Please, please be with me." Suddenly, there was a break in the clouds. The sun lit up the sky and a beautiful rainbow appeared. I'm sure that to many people the rainbow was simply a beautiful sight. But to me it was an answer. It was a confirmation of God's presence in my life.

❖ *Beloved Friend, you received my covenant sign to you today! There was a time when you would not have noticed my rainbow. But now you understand the rainbow's meaning. You knew it was from me and received my gift of comfort. Your journey through grief has taught you to see the signs of my love that are there for you all along the way.*

*I was sleeping, but my heart kept vigil.*
Song of Songs 5:2

❖ Our love song goes on. I find myself remembering him in the ordinary events of our days together. Tucking our children in at night; picking the season's first tomatoes, the cup of tea in the evening; the friends around our table. In all these ways and countless others, I remember him. I can no longer touch him, but my heart knows he is still there for me.

❖ *Dear Heart, you have plumbed the depths of my love which lives forever. It is the greatest of my gifts to each of you and knows no boundaries. Keep vigil in your heart and let this love go out to others who need your gentle touch.*

*Voices of Grief*

*Then your light shall break forth like the dawn,
and your wound shall quickly be healed.*
Isaiah 58:8

❖ I breakfast alone in my quiet kitchen. Some mornings I am at peace. I savor the coming day, enjoy my coffee, make my lists. Other mornings I am restless. My spirit is ill at ease in the quiet. I long for a banged back door, a blast of radio music, a car horn beeping in the driveway. My cereal tastes like paper; the coffee I pour grows cold in my cup. It is as if the sun touches my world with its bright light on some mornings and on others, the sunlight cannot penetrate the gray cloud around me.

❖ *Dear Friend, faith is knowing that the sun is always there even when it is hidden behind a cloud. Life will never be without its clouds until you are home with me at last. Only remember that you have seen the sun. Your wound is healing. Put your trust in me, for I am your sunlight. Be as faithful as the little basket of violets on your kitchen window sill allowing the sunlight to coax their exquisite bright flowers into bloom.*

*He has sent me to bring glad tidings to the lowly, to heal the brokenhearted.*
Isaiah 61:1

❖ Just last year her birthday cake was the center of attention. We decided to put all 50 candles on it and let them blaze away! Our friends were there and celebrated with us. I'm so glad she let us do that. Who would have guessed it would be her last birthday party? Tonight our friends are taking me out for a quiet dinner. I don't want to go, but I feel their need to be together this way and I will do this for them.

❖ *My Child, relax tonight in the comfort that only dear friends can offer one another. Let them tell their stories of her and she will be among you again. You are hungry to talk about her, to remember her, to honor her. In gathering to extend love and comfort, you are healing each other. We shall be there with you, she and I, and bring you our comfort and peace.*

*Voices of Grief*

*But store up treasures in heaven, where neither moth nor decay destroys, nor thieves break in and steal. For where your treasure is, there also will your heart be.*
Matthew 6:20

❖ Today is the feast of All Souls. I am at the park sitting by the lake and thinking of each of them, family members and friends, who are my treasures in heaven. I call each by name and cast an autumn leaf upon the water. The water carries each leaf away on a journey into the heart of the lake, into the heart of God. May they rest in the palm of his hand and know only love and peace.

❖ *Dear One, when you enter this life, your final journey will be made in the company of many loved ones. They will surround you with golden light and you will experience a joy such as you have never known before.*

*Coming Home*

*Blessed are they who mourn,
for they will be comforted.*
Matthew 5:4

❖ Thanksgiving is my favorite holiday. She knew that I delighted in the "gathering in" of people at the harvest time of year. My harvest is my family, my children and grandchildren. My table is the altar around which we gather. We join hands and count our blessings. I thank God for her . . . their mother and grandmother, my wife. We add the names of those who have been called away from our table. We light the candles, tell the stories and ignite a late November afternoon with eternal love.

❖ *Dear Friend, the glow of your Thanksgiving love goes directly to my heart. Be assured that your special family garden continues to grow and yield a rich harvest.*

*Voices of Grief*

*The daybreak from on high will visit us*
*to shine on those who sit in darkness*
*and death's shadow,*
*to guide our feet into the path of peace.*
Luke 1:78-79

❖ It is a fine late October day. A long summer drought threatened to limit the display of fall color this year. Instead, the weather stayed mild and rain began falling in such abundance that the reservoirs are brimming again and every tree is aflame with autumn color. The expected dusty fall with dry, brown leaves has been transformed. Rain and sun have brought forth the beauty that lay hidden in the heart of each leaf. Maybe I see her ever more clearly because her memory is like these leaves, watered by my tears and burning deep within my heart.

❖ *Dear Heart, I shine my light of love, faith and hope on you daily. Those beautiful leaves are but tiny sparks in the glowing spectrum of my love for you. Let these thoughts of changing seasons and the constantly turning earth give you peace. For I am there ordering all life and bidding you to turn to me in trust again and again.*

*Coming Home*

*I am the bread of life; whoever comes to me will never hunger, and whoever believes in me will never thirst.*
John 6:35

❖ I dismissed my grandfather's faith as old country religion complete with fear, guilt, and superstition. I saw only the negatives and didn't realize until now that his faith was deep, abiding, and very real. Mass and Holy Communion were a true source of strength to him, even when his mind was failing. I can still see him waiting for his friends outside his church. Stiffened, bent, leaning on canes, they made their way up the center aisle together for Mass. Then they went out to breakfast to solve the mysteries of their lives. If only I could call him now that I understand. . . .

❖ *Precious Friend, he knows. Both of you wanted to love and be at peace, and in that desire, I was present. It is time to look at today and to look ahead. What can you do to feed those who are hungry for the good news of eternal life? Honor your grandfather's memory by loving and accepting those around you.*

*Voices of Grief*

*Do not work for food that perishes but for the food that endures for eternal life, which the Son of Man will give you. For on him the Father, God, has set his seal.*
John 6:27

❖ Preparing Christmas dinner was the same every year. It would always be at Mom's house and we daughters and daughters-in-law would work together, cooking and setting the table as beautifully as we could. Our background music was Mom's laughter, answered by our own. Nothing could have prepared me for the lonely shock of preparing Christmas dinner alone in my own quiet kitchen as I do now. The last time we shared the joy of Christmas dinner with Mom was many years ago and it lives in my heart as if it were yesterday afternoon.

❖ *Beloved, your hands peeled potatoes and stirred gravy, but your hearts were storing the treasure of your family love in my heavenly home. Your mother's laughter is my delight. Share your own love and laughter as food for the spirits of those who need my nourishment today.*

*It is the spirit that gives life, while the flesh is of no avail. The words I have spoken to you are spirit and life.*
John 6:63

❖ Oh, how we loved to sail together! I would cast off the lines and push off from the dock. Then with the tiller in his capable hands, we would fall off the wind and fill up our sails. With a snap, the wind would propel our little boat out into the river. It was exhilarating to hold those lines in our hands and feel the power of that invisible force. Laughing like little children, we would try to outrun another boat and outguess the wind. Spirit and breath and wind . . . the very air powering our lives together, filling our sails and sending us flying to a stronger truth.

❖ *Dear Heart, that wonderful freedom is born of trust. You believed in a power you couldn't see and grew to understand its workings in your life. Now, you are experiencing the Spirit of my love in a new way. What you two discovered together is now your truth to share with others.*

*Voices of Grief*

> *Whoever drinks the water I shall give will never thirst; the water I shall give will become in him a spring of water welling up to eternal life.*
> John 4:14

❖ Our family vacation was always spent at the beach, until the year our daughter died and none of us could face going without her. Oh, how she loved the beach! Now that we're here again, we see her everywhere. It is almost as if we have been given back a small measure of her presence in a place where her memory is strong and good.

❖ *Dear Friend, continue to say yes to life. You have all been renewed in the past by the rhythm of the sea and the light sparkling on the waves. You needed to allow that gift back into your hearts. For along with the tranquility of the shore, you allowed my life and hers to enter and refresh your thirsty spirits again.*

*He will wipe every tear from their eyes, and there shall be no more death or mourning, or wailing or pain.*
Revelation 21:4

❖ I had the dancing dream again last night. There is a vast, gray place where people are moving round and round in a circle dance. They hold hands but their eyes are closed and they appear to be dancing in their sleep. It is a disturbing dream, because the dancers are joined together but remain completely isolated from one another.

❖ *Precious Friend, the dancers are those who have not yet let me touch them. Their tears lie unshed in their closed eyes. They live in a twilight land where they turn round and round and do not know and trust their destination or each other. I will open their eyes, and I invite you to walk directly toward me, toward the light. Your tears will fall, but I will wipe them from your cheeks and pour my joy into your heart.*

*Voices of Grief*

> *The favors of the LORD are not exhausted,*
> *his mercies are not spent;*
> *They are renewed each morning,*
> *so great is his faithfulness.*
> *My portion is the LORD, says my soul;*
> *therefore will I hope in him.*
> Lamentations 3:22-24

❖ Ah, the sun peeks into my window at last! I've been waiting here for the daybreak, for God's first light to awaken the earth. Now, my day can begin. Who will God send to me today? I am already praying for them, these unknown people who need to be touched by my old hands. I just ask him to hold my dear departed family and friends in the palm of his hand. The Lord is so good! I trust him totally to strengthen me for the work of the day.

❖ *My Dear Child, I hear your song of love and praise this morning with great joy. You shall be my hands and heart today and you shall feel a measure of the joy I feel in your generous spirit. I hold your dear ones constantly in my embrace.*

*Choose life, then, that you and your descendants may live.*
Deuteronomy 30:19

❖ These words are so painful to me. If I choose life, does it mean that I will forget my loved one? Must I choose life with all those words imply . . . planning my future, painting the house, cooking, planting seeds . . . not merely existing, but living again?

❖ *"I choose life." My child, whisper these words to me now. I will carry you in my arms through the day. And as you continue to choose life, you will come to know a quickening in your heart. You will walk forward on your own. First, as one moving in a dream and then with stronger strides. As a child crawls, then walks and runs, so, too, will you embrace life again.*

*Voices of Grief*

> *What I say to you in the darkness, speak in the light; what you hear whispered, proclaim on the housetops.*
> Matthew 10:27

❖ I let the evening gather about me last night. As it grew dark, I sat on in my rocking chair. I didn't switch on the lights and the 6 o'clock news as I usually do. I didn't start dinner. I rocked. I stared into the dark and my eyes were drawn to the street light glowing feebly outside my window. Tears rolled down my cheeks. My throat ached and my chest heaved with sobs. I called her name. I blamed God. I let all my defenses down. Then I felt a warmth and peace envelope my spirit.

❖ *Dear Heart, you were finally quiet enough to hear my whisper, empty enough to notice my presence. I've been with you all along. But you must look beyond your ordinary routine to touch the promise of eternity. Listen in the quiet space within and you will know I am near.*

*Kindness and truth shall meet;*
*Justice and peace shall kiss.*
*Truth shall spring out of the earth,*
*And Justice shall look down from heaven.*
Psalm 85:11-12

❖ Oh, God, I think of her in the morning as I start my day. Only you know how I long to meet her again; hold her and kiss her again. You are the God who made us and gave us to each other. I live my life, but I am aware now of another, and greater, reality than the one I see all around me each day. She waits for me there with you.

❖ *Dear Friend, I know the agony of human separation. My cross taught me its pain and my resurrection banished it forever. In my kingdom you shall know only kindness, truth, justice, peace, and, over all, love.*

*Voices of Grief*

> *Take off your robe of mourning and misery;*
> *put on the splendor of glory from God forever . . .*
> *Led away on foot by their enemies they left you:*
> *but God will bring them back to you*
> *borne aloft in glory as on royal thrones.*
> Baruch 5:1,6

❖ There, the last box is packed away and my tears are spent. Everyone has been telling me to put his things away. Clean out his room. Get rid of his clothes. I needed to wait. I needed time to get used to this last goodbye. I am so grateful, God, that I listened to my heart. I saved very little . . . just enough to remind me of the special moments and to give me something of his to touch.

❖ *Beloved, you have journeyed far in this time of mourning and made your painful peace with separation. And your dear one, who left his earthly garments behind, is arrayed in glory and waits for you here in the splendor of my kingdom.*

*But the souls of the just are in the hand of God,
and no torment shall touch them.*
Wisdom 3:1

❖ My God, when I think of all the time since she died I wonder at the effort it has taken me to keep my anger and hurt alive. I realized today that she is at peace. At last, I am begging for a measure of that peace for myself.

❖ *Yes, Dear Child, it is time for you, too, to be at peace. In many ways your hurt has sustained you through this time of loss. Now it is time to move beyond that existence. Remember, where I am there is no torment. Open your heart in peace and love and allow me to dwell there at the center of your being.*

*Voices of Grief*

> *They were all astounded and glorified God, saying, "We have never seen anything like this."*
> Mark 2:12

❖ Bit by bit, I am unclenching my hands. All my life I have tried to control, manage, protect. If I just held on tightly enough, everything would be all right. Now I know it is not about escaping the pain of human life, but counting on God's love to overcome that pain.

❖ *Precious Friend, I have been waiting with open arms for you. Now, you will know my presence in your life. Trust in me and you, too, will say that you have never seen anything like this. You will actually come back to life and see its beauty again.*

*New wine is poured into fresh wineskins.*
Mark 2:22

❖ I have been pressed down by sorrow, my God. Today has been a day like so many others, filled with the struggle to survive his death. My former life is no more. I often still yearn for its peace; I know that I can't go back.

❖ *You have withstood the tribulation of death, Dear Heart. In a sense when he died, you died, too. You died to the familiar ways of your comfortable life. You have had to relinquish the childish faith you counted on to protect yourself . . . almost like a good luck charm. You now understand a new faith that experiences the pain of letting go and still believes that life continues in a new way. This is a part of every human life, even my own. The difference I have made is that I will never leave you alone. I will love and live with you forever. I will be the new wine in the fresh wineskin of your life.*

*Voices of Grief*

> *What I say to you, I say to all: "Watch!"*
> Mark 13:37

❖ He had gone out to work among his beloved flowers. It was a late summer afternoon and he was going to pick roses for our dinner table. When I walked out with a cool drink for him, he was already dead. We had no warning; no hint of his vulnerability. We lived our lives each day as best we could. I have wished so often that we could have said goodbye.

❖ *I remember, Dear Heart. He slipped away amidst the beauty of his flowers. I see you sitting there on the garden bench. I hear your thoughts and prayers for him and all your beloved, departed ones. You will know when it is your time that he has been sitting with you each day. You will know amazement and delight at the wonders the garden of paradise holds for you.*

*He is not the God of the dead but of the living.*
Mark 12:27

❖ For a long time the readings, homilies, and hymns at Sunday Mass were just words to me. But lately I have noticed I feel a powerful sense of peace when I listen. It happens especially when I am praying for her, or telling her I love her, or asking her opinion about our children. I have no doubt that she lives.

❖ *Those who seem to be dead, Dear Friend, are abiding with me. There are only living beings in my kingdom. Some have fallen asleep; some still walk the earth. I am the God of all. You have only to call my name and I will answer.*

*Voices of Grief*

*If your whole body is full of light, and no part of it is in darkness, then it will be as full of light as a lamp illuminating you with its brightness.*
Luke 11:36

❖ The waves lapping at my toes today are like liquid crystal. The sunlight is clear, sharp, and strong late on this August afternoon. My beach umbrella casts its patch of shade and I notice that the air is too cool in its shadow. So I venture forth again to the sunny sand to warm up. The bright August sunlight penetrates my skin with its heat and my spirit with its fiery beauty. God, you know how much he would have loved such a day!

❖ *Fill yourself with light, Beloved. I desire that you burn brightly with the flame of my eternal love.*

*He was carried away by angels to the bosom of Abraham.*
Luke 16:22

❖ I went to the movies alone tonight. When my friends couldn't go, I decided I would go alone. I am so proud of myself and he would be, too. He always wanted me to try new things. Since his death, the list of things I have had to learn to do is long. But this is different. I went to that movie for the sheer pleasure of it. It lifted my spirit and I felt his hand on my shoulder.

❖ *Dear Heart, my angels carry you, too. They are with you as you begin to follow your heart and listen to your own needs. I long to see you whole again. You are a new creation who has weathered the storm and stands before me renewed.*

*Voices of Grief*

*What are you discussing as you walk along?*
Luke 24:17

❖ Ahh . . . that's better. Just to hold and soothe these little ones is to be close to the heart of God. I have learned to speak God's love with my body. It is truly amazing how he has filled up my empty arms. I kiss the tops of curly brown heads and rest my cheek on blond ringlets. They're all the same to me . . . God's littlest angels in need of my arms.

❖ *Beloved, I hold you in the same way. You have chosen to walk along giving love and comfort to my children, the least in my kingdom. My head bends tenderly to yours as I kiss the lonely place in your soul.*

*Our days are like the grass;
like flowers of the field we blossom;
The wind sweeps over us and we are gone.
Our place knows us no more.*
Psalm 103:15-16

❖ God, I am an old man now. All my friends are gone. When I make my way to the park in the afternoon, the bench we shared for years is empty. Oh, the men who still come to gossip and play checkers are good men, but I miss my old friends. There's no one here who knew my Mary.

❖ *Beloved Friend, the place that you and your Mary and your friends enjoyed together in the park will be empty, but your life will be full in a way you can only dream of now. Your span of years on earth runs its course and is no more, but eternal life is the life I will share with you. It is your family, your friends, and your Mary ageless as the angels and sheltered in my arms.*

*Voices of Grief*

> *When you were younger, you used to dress yourself and go where you wanted; but when you grow old, you will stretch out your hands, and someone else will dress you and lead you where you do not want to go.*
> John 21:18

❖ God, I think now of my father at the convalescent center he never left alive. He was so confused and would always ask, "where am I sleeping tonight?" I came to understand that his confusion was a freedom for him. He wasn't aware that he was no longer independent. Together we preserved his dignity, he and I, and distilled our relationship to its essence: love.

❖ *Dear One, your father ascended his own cross and endured its suffering with great patience. You held the cup to his lips and relieved his pain and confusion as best you could. There is a fierce and wonderful beauty in such human dignity as was his. He has put aside his cross and dwells with me in glory.*

*Coming Home*

*Stay with us, for it is nearly evening and the day is almost over.*
Luke 24:29

Dear Little Sis,
I have walked on alone. It is one year today since I held your hand and let you go. I guess you know how often I've thought of you. Today will be a special day. I'm going to celebrate you with the joy you always brought to life. I'm going to walk on the beach and find a perfect little shell to put on the chain I wear around my neck. I'll have shrimp for lunch . . . your favorite. I'll lay a daisy wreath on your grave and toast you at sunset. Then I'll light a candle and sit quietly in its glow at the end of our special day. Be with me.
         Love always,
         Your Big Sis

❖ *Beloved, I know how difficult the past year has been for you to bear, but you have turned to me and together we have continued the journey. I have carried you in my arms.*

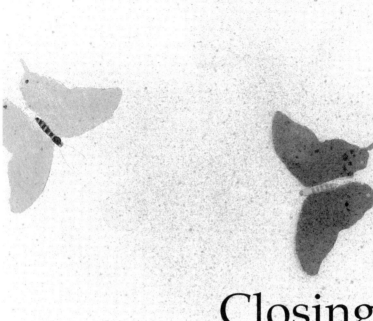

# Closing

*I have called you by name;
   you are mine.*
      Isaiah 43:1

*Closing*

# Honor Your Loved One/Honor Yourself

The time will come as you journey down the long road of grief when the clouds begin to part. It is as if the sun has broken through a murky gray sky. There is a sense of renewed energy and an increased desire to mark the moments of your life together in a special way. Throughout the journey you have been remembering the sacred moments of the life you shared. Here are some suggested ways to honor your loved one and to honor your own strength and courage on the journey. You may already have many such rituals incorporated into your own life. This list is meant to supplement your own efforts to honor the gift of life.

*Plant a Garden*

Be it a dish garden or an area outdoors where you can name the place for your loved one. Plant several varieties of seeds or plants, perhaps, your loved one's favorites. If possible place a bench or chair where you can sit quietly and reflect, surrounded by these reminders of Resurrection. Make a sign which bears your loved one's name and dedicate this holy ground.

*Listen to Music*

Make a special quiet time to play your old shared favorites. Or you may want to listen to music which has the capacity to soothe and create the peaceful setting for meditation. Your spirit will be given the opportunity to let go as you pray and remember.

*Choose a Small Action and Act*

If you are ready, it may be time to volunteer to help in your church or local community. Any effort, however

*Voices of Grief*

small, is much needed and will give you the opportunity to reach out to others. Read to a child, bake cookies, take care of someone, take care of yourself.

*Adopt a Pet*
Bring new life into your home for companionship. Pets are fine listeners and unstinting bestowers of love.

*Walk by the Water*
If you are blessed with a pond, lake, stream, or ocean nearby, go there often. Walk or sit near the water's edge and let your mind wander. Allow the peace of the place to penetrate your being. And even if your spirit is not peaceful, you will be encouraged to express your feelings by the gentle, soothing movement of the water itself. If you are landlocked, choose a particular feature of the landscape and make it yours. A grassy hill, beautiful tree, the sunset, a stained glass window—any of these can function as a focal point of peace and give you time and space for quiet reflection.

*Tender Loving Care*
Shop, have a message, play golf, visit a museum, see a play. It is vital that you take care of your own physical and emotional needs in small, positive ways. It doesn't have to be an extravagant gesture. A simple lunch in the park or a new hair cut may be all it takes to honor and care for yourself today.

*Make Something/Build Something*
A plant stand, book shelf, new curtains, an apple pie. Call up your creative, nurturing instinct that abides deep within you. Your mind, hands, and heart will be

*Closing*

occupied and you will have produced something to remind yourself that you are healing.

*Go for a Walk*

After dinner this evening, when the day is over and the light of the sunset is bathing the earth, go outside and walk around the block. Really notice the evening.

*Breathe Deeply*

Sit up straight in your chair and draw the breath of life deep within your body. Feel your abdomen expand as you inhale and contract as you exhale. Do this two or three times and notice how deep breathing can calm you and bring you peace. Throughout the day take time to become aware of your breath and its gift of life.

*Go Fishing*

Go back to the water again but this time bring a fishing pole, a book, and a picnic lunch. You may catch fish or not, but you will spend quiet time outdoors renewing and refreshing your spirit.

*Write Your Story*

Write down a favorite memory of your loved one. Tell the story of your life together; tell the story of your life apart.

*Bake Bread*

Baking bread is its own reward. The very act is therapeutic and the results are nourishment for body and soul. Bread will not assume its shape and size if it isn't kneaded first. And in the kneading is the therapy. As you fold and pound the dough, you will use physical and

*Voices of Grief*

and emotional energy. Best of all is the quiet moment of enjoying the wonderful taste and aroma of fresh, baked bread—a treat for body, mind, and spirit.

*Collect Poetry*

Poems express our deepest longings and most intense emotions. You will recognize your own thoughts and feelings in a poet's words. It helps to know that you are in touch with the universal experience of humankind. It also helps to know that somebody could express these feelings in beautiful, evocative language. Find your favorite poems and take comfort from them often.

*Write a Poem*

Try your own hand at poetry. This spare and rhythmic way of expressing yourself may help you sort out your journey, both the path you walked together and the one you now walk alone.

*Read the Bible*

Sacred Scripture is the voice of our God. Open the Bible and read from the Old or New Testament. Let its language enter your heart. Know that this is a living family story and that you are a treasured member of God's family.

*Exercise*

Your lowest priority may be your own physical well-being. But it is known that exercise revitalizes body and soul, giving extra strength and renewed energy. You may find a half hour of exercise routines to follow on videotape or television or you may want to investigate programs offered by your local community center or health club.

*Closing*

The simple act of taking a walk can help you begin to experience the benefits of increased physical activity. Honor yourself by taking good care of yourself.

*Write a Letter*

A note or letter is good way to communicate, even with someone who lives nearby, when you are not up to seeing them. Or send a card if that is all you can manage. For now, let the greeting card speak for you. It is the simple act of staying in touch, that will encourage you and your friend. As you feel ready to write letters, you will know the satisfaction of expressing your thoughts and feelings on paper.

*Crochet, Knit, or Craft*

Start with a small project. Something you can work on at home or carry with you. Maybe a piece of counted cross stitch would appeal to you. Or knit or crochet a scarf to keep a special child warm this winter. The list of possible projects is unlimited—dry some flowers from your garden and create a wreath; mount and frame a special photograph.

*Visit Memory Lane*

Take out your photo albums and travel again through your days and years together. Memories of your loved one can never be lost. The time you spent together can't be taken from you. If your photos are simply in a box or drawer, this may be the time to organize them and place them in albums. That way they will be easy for you to see and share with friends and family.

*Voices of Grief*

*Ask For Stories*

When people say that they don't know how to help you or are afraid they may hurt you by saying the wrong thing, ask them to share their memories of your loved one. The stories they tell are pieces of the fabric of your loved one's life and your own life. Many stories you will have heard before; many will be new to you. But in the retelling of the stories lies the important act of remembering the beloved.

*Make Lists*

Write down the places you visited; the games you enjoyed playing, the restaurants you frequented; the movies that were special favorites. Write down the places you dreamed of going; the plans you had for the future. Think of the things on the list that you can still hope to do. Plan to fulfill some of the dreams you dreamed together in honor of your loved one. When you are ready to make plans again, you may make a new list of the dreams you now dream for yourself.